Celestial Embers in the Night

Stars giggle in the dark sky,
They wink like they know the why.
A moonbeam slips on a banana peel,
Laughing at shadows that twirl and wheel.

The comets throw a cosmic dance,
While planets wear their best pants.
Asteroids shout, 'Don't take it too hard!'
Even black holes find time to guard.

The Unfading Dawn

Roosters crow as the sun yawns wide,
It stretches out, the night tucked inside.
The coffee pot sings a happy tune,
While lazy cats bask in the afternoon.

Morning squirrels do acrobatic flips,
Chasing each other and stealing chips.
A rainbow slips on its morning shoes,
Coloring the day with vibrant hues.

Illuminated Echoes of Tomorrow

Flickering lights hum a tiny song,
Echoes of laughter, like where they belong.
The future chats with a cup of tea,
'Is it the milk, or just my glee?'

Tomorrow peeks through a window crack,
Whispering secrets, then fades back.
A toaster pops, it's toast on a spree,
Dancing on counters, what a jubilee!

Beyond the Boundless Bright

In the land where giggles explode,
Sunflowers wear hats to lighten the load.
The clouds paint pictures with fluffy gray,
While rainbows take turns to play all day.

Unicorns prank the passing breeze,
Sprinkling glitter like it's cheese.
The horizon's always just plain fun,
Chasing the laughter that never is done.

Beacon of the Universe

In the sky, a winking star,
Waving like a weird bazaar.
It beams and shakes, its glow's a tease,
Calling cats and dogs with ease.

The aliens giggle, what a sight,
Dancing under the cosmic light.
They roast marshmallows on a spark,
While making jokes in the dark.

A comet zooms, then takes a bow,
As if to say, 'Look at me now!'
The universe winks, what a show,
It's a playful dance, let it flow.

With every flash, we laugh out loud,
Underneath this twinkling shroud.
Who knew that space could be so fun?
Join the laugh; we've just begun!

The Infinite Gleam

A firefly joins the nightly race,
Its flicker looks like a happy face.
It flits around, teasing the moon,
Making wishes in a joyful tune.

Stars trade secrets, giggles in flight,
They very much enjoy the night.
One cheeky star ate too much pie,
And now it rolls across the sky!

Galaxies swirl in a silly dance,
A cosmic party—take a chance!
With every sparkle, a joke unfolds,
A humorous tale that never grows old.

Laughter rings where shadows retreat,
In this brightness, life is sweet.
Join the jest, join the spree,
In this endless giggle, come and see!

The Ever-Burning Flame

A candle flickers on the table,
Wobbling like a charade fable.
It lights the room with goofy grace,
Dulling all worries in its space.

With every bounce and silly sway,
It winks hello, come join the play.
A moth shows up to steal its glow,
But the flame just laughs, 'You're too slow!'

Friends gather round for a funny tale,
While shadows dance like ships at sail.
The flame sizzles, like popcorn on the stove,
Each laugh a spark, each smile a grove.

So come, my friend, stay for the fun,
As we toast to laughter, one by one.
In this warm circle, we rise and cheer,
For a flame that glows, making all clear!

Twilight's Embrace

When day bids night a funny cheer,
Colors blend in a wacky sphere.
The sun makes faces, the moon just grins,
As twilight waltzes and spins.

Crickets play their tiny strings,
While fireflies don their golden rings.
The sky bursts with colors, red and blue,
In this playful concert, join the crew!

Clouds morph into shapes of delight,
A dragon here, a goat in flight.
They share jokes, oh what a sight,
Laughter echoing through the night.

So grab a friend, embrace the dusk,
In these giggles, let love be the musk.
For in twilight's arms, with every spark,
We find the humor hiding in the dark!

Illuminated Realms

In a land where the sun eats pie,
Dancing shadows leap and fly.
The stars in hats and quirky shoes,
Whisper tales of cosmic blues.

The moon plays chess with a cunning fox,
Time slips by in mismatched socks.
The lightbulbs giggle, shining bright,
As we chase fireflies in a flight.

A rainbow's laugh upon the ground,
Sparks of joy in every sound.
With every giggle, the colors collide,
Painting laughter from side to side.

So here we frolic, twist and twirl,
In these realms where light's a swirl.
With each silly step, a new delight,
We dance together, hearts in flight.

The Glow of Forever

There's a lamp that claims to be profound,
In a treasure chest beneath the mound.
It hums like bees, it glows like cheese,
Making wishes float upon the breeze.

Chickens tell jokes to the rising sun,
While squirrels skate at the merry fun.
The laughter echoes from head to toe,
In this glow, who wouldn't want to know?

A disco ball hangs from an old oak tree,
Reflecting giggles, wild and free.
The fireflies twirl with sparkly cheer,
Creating a party that draws us near.

So if you seek a place to cheer,
Come dance with shadows, have no fear.
In the glow where time stands still,
You'll find your heart with a playful thrill.

Radiant Reflections

Mirrors laugh, they twist and bend,
Making faces that never end.
With every glance, a new surprise,
You might just see a cat in disguise.

Toasters pop resembling stars,
Toast struts out with shiny cars.
Jam jars sing in a pickle jar way,
As we groove on this funny display.

Puddles giggle, splashing around,
Dancing shoes on the muddy ground.
With each reflection, a silly glance,
Encouraging us all to dance.

So plunge into the shiny maze,
Get lost in laughter, in this daze.
Here, every sparkle shows its might,
In the realm of radiant, funny light.

Celestial Journeys

In rocket ships made of candy floss,
We zoom through space with a giggle toss.
Stars wear pajamas, twinkling bright,
Singing songs that dance in the night.

Planets trade hats like a board game,
Jupiter spins, but never gets lame.
We chase comets on a silly ride,
Through cosmic clouds, we slide and glide.

Black holes joke, saying, "Come on in!"
But don't stay long, or you cannot win.
The universe laughs with each tick-tock,
As we surf the waves of a time-block.

So pack your giggles, let's take flight,
In journeys where everything is light.
With friends and laughter, we'll hold on tight,
For the joy of a journey is pure delight.

The Dawn's Promise

As the sun peeks, a wink so bright,
Birds in chorus, a morning delight.
Coffee spills as the mug takes flight,
A dance of joy, in soft daylight.

Chasing shadows, we all take a race,
Tripping over dreams, a silly embrace.
Monkeys in pajamas, oh, what a place!
Life's silly moments, we happily chase.

Transcendent Gleam

Shiny spoons and forks have a glow,
Dancing in kitchens, they put on a show.
Mice in tuxedos, with tails in tow,
Join the party, what a funny flow!

Whiskers twitching, the cat joins the spree,
Chasing the sunbeam, oh, let it be free!
With giggles and purrs, we laugh with glee,
Such radiant moments, a sight to see!

Celestial Pathways

Stars have socks, hung up on the line,
Winking and sparkling, they're feeling fine.
Mice in space, sipping cheese and wine,
Floating on giggles, what a great sign!

Galaxies spin with a tickle and tease,
While comets blast off with the greatest ease.
Juggling moons, like big beach ball trees,
Bouncing through laughter, oh, what a breeze!

The Everlasting Glimmer

Lightning bugs in a disco jam,
Twinkling together, oh stampede of glam.
Frogs in bow ties, croaking the program,
Jumping and bouncing, a glitch in the grand!

Rainbows slide down the shimmering stream,
Chasing each other, a colorful dream.
With splashes of color, hear the laughter beam,
It's all just a joke, or so it would seem!

A Beacon in the Starlit Sea

A lighthouse laughs at the waves,
With a wink and a quirky shine,
It dances with the fish below,
Sipping moonlight like fine wine.

The seagulls squawk jokes to the breeze,
While crabs tell tales with a clap,
Beneath the glow of a giggling star,
They throw a nightly crabby rap.

Boats drift by with silly grins,
Chasing echoes of echoing chimes,
As jellyfish juggle in the dark,
And time skips like flipped rhyming rhymes.

The Unyielding Glow of Dreams

Pillows fluff with whispered wishes,
As moonbeams tickle sleepy heads,
The dreams parade with silly hats,
Creating giggles in our beds.

A unicorn wearing polka dots,
Invites a turtle to a race,
While fairies spread confetti dreams,
In an ever-dancing space.

Laughter echoing through the night,
As teddy bears conspire and plot,
With adventures waiting in their hugs,
They shine in blankets, cool and hot.

Shimmering Pathways of Forever

The sidewalk glows with painted stars,
Where shadows tap their little feet,
A parade of giggles strolls along,
Where even the pavement's got a beat.

The moon is a playful giant,
Playing tag with clouds and dreams,
As fireworks in puffy hats,
Burst with joy in colorful beams.

Sneakers squeak like happy mice,
Spreading sparkles on the route,
With laughter making echoes sing,
And fireflies join the joyful suit.

Light's Embrace at the Edge of Dusk

The sun waves bye with a cheeky grin,
While crickets prepare for a concert,
The sky throws on its evening dress,
In hues that make the stars convert.

Silly shadows stretch and yawn,
Doing the limbo on the grass,
While a chubby cat serenades,
In a dreamy, fuzzy mass.

As fireflies join the dance of dusk,
With arms like ribbons, they twirl around,
And the world chuckles in delight,
In this glow, absurdly profound.

Horizon of Hope

The sun forgot to set today,
It's shining through my window pane.
I tried to cook but burned the toast,
Yet here I am, a brightness host.

My cat is plotting with the beam,
She pounces hard; it's quite the theme.
She dashes here, she dances there,
A furry comet in the air.

The shadows giggle, chase their tails,
As laughter drifts upon the gales.
In this odd light, we trip and steer,
What fun it is to disappear!

Chasing the Radiance

I saw a glow beneath the bed,
I thought it was a taco spread!
But, alas, it was my shoes instead,
Reflecting all the crumbs I dread.

I chased a glow upon the floor,
What's that? A sock? A shiny door?
I stumbled on a puppy's toy,
And my dance turned to a ploy.

The room now twinkles with delight,
Like fireflies in the dead of night.
I laugh and leap, my feet take flight,
No taco here, just pure daylight!

Timeless Glistening

My grandma's necklace sparkles bright,
She claims it's from an alien flight.
I wear it proudly, feeling grand,
'Till it slips off, right from my hand!

It bounces off the fridge, a ping,
The dog looks up as if to sing.
He cocks his head; it catches light,
And suddenly, he's a star tonight!

With every gleam, my hopes take wing,
A dishes-clanging, joyful thing.
We dance along the shining rays,
And laugh away our silly days!

Eternal Echoes of Light

I saw a flicker in the stew,
Thought it was magic, maybe too!
But no, a spoon's reflection played,
And now it calls—what have I made?

Time was stuck in this bright soup,
I joined a jig with a cucumber troupe.
They danced around my kitchen floor,
No recipe, just joy galore!

Each echo of a laugh and glare,
Bounced off walls and filled the air.
With each bright wink, I stomped a beat,
My bubbling stew became a treat!

Light Beyond Time

In the fridge, there's a glow so bright,
Leftover pizza takes flight at night.
The cat thinks it's a UFO,
Hovering there with a cheesy hello.

Socks lost in the laundry vortex spin,
Shining like stars, they try to get in.
Yet they vanish, those mischievous thieves,
A comedy skit that no one believes.

The clock laughs at us, ticks with glee,
Each second a joke, wild and free.
Time's a magician with endless tricks,
Making minutes do acrobatics and flips.

So here's to the light that plays alongside,
Dancing in shadows, it won't abide.
Humor shines with no boundaries seen,
In the quirkiest moments, oh so serene.

The Continuum of Shine

A bulb flickers, life's little tease,
Making us guess, with a flick of the keys.
It glows with a grin, as if to say,
'What's a lightbulb without a little play?'

The sun yawns wide, rises with flair,
Chasing away the snooze-fest despair.
With sunglasses on, it's ready to beam,
Mimicking stars in a daytime dream.

Moonbeams giggle, slipping on ice,
Trying to skate, oh, isn't it nice?
They trip on their glow, bump the old trees,
Sharing the laughter, if you please!

So let's bask in this shiny spree,
Where every ray brings absurdity.
In the continuum where all sense blurs,
Keep shining, dear friend, with no detours.

Ethereal Beacons

The firefly dances in a wild rave,
A disco ball in nature's cave.
Flickering wings, they form a cue,
Telling the frogs, 'We're here for you!'

Stars prance on the canvas, quite bold,
Winking at dreams, like secrets told.
They throw a party in the night sky,
With comets as guests, oh my, oh my!

The lighthouse beams a quirky grin,
Waving at ships like, 'Come on in!'
But they might get lost in the beam's embrace,
A nautical fool's race, just in case.

So shine we must in this slapstick play,
Where jokes are bright and troubles sway.
Ethereal beacons, a whimsical crew,
Lighting the way for the jesters too.

The Brilliance of Forever

In a world where light has a silly plan,
Shining like disco in a glow-worm van.
The sun and moon debate in jest,
Who's shining brightest? A funny quest!

A glowworm graduates with honors so grand,
'Look at me!' it shouts, lamps in hand.
But ants run off, not a moment to spare,
Chasing the light, unaware of the flare.

Every spark has a story to tell,
Of comical moments when all's gone swell.
So let's raise a toast to the long-lasting,
Brilliance of laughter, forever casting.

With fun in our hearts and a wink of fate,
Let's ride the rays, it's never too late.
For in this glow, we'll always be bright,
Wrapped in the joy of whimsical light!

Luminescent Dreams

In the sky, a glow so bright,
A moth's dance at half-past night.
It twirls around a buzzing bee,
Singing songs of glee and spree.

A cat in shades, with shades askew,
Claims the moon, says, "It's my due!"
The stars wink back with cheeky smiles,
While time flies softly for a while.

Balloons are floating, quite absurd,
They whisper soft and silly words.
A rabbit hops in silver shoes,
While giggling gently, spreading hues.

So here we are, in colors spun,
Beneath a giggling silver sun.
The dreams we chase, both wild and free,
In this silly glow, it's just you and me.

Infinity's Song

A banana slips, it starts to hum,
While dancing with a great big drum.
The cherries giggle every beat,
Tap-dancing in a merry feat.

An owl wears socks, both mismatched,
On this stage, no one's dispatched.
A chicken clucks a serenade,
While shadows prance in bright cascade.

The clouds make shapes, a dog, a cat,
And giggle at a silly hat.
Infinity twirls on a teetering stage,
As laughter echoes, chasing rage.

Hold on tight, for the ride is steep,
In this zany world, we'll take a leap.
Without a care, we'll sing along,
In the glow of our infinity's song.

Eternal Gleam

A lightbulb flickers with a grin,
A quirky dance about to begin.
A squirrel in a traffic cone,
Claims it's his luxurious throne.

The sun peeks in, a cheeky tease,
While shadows giggle in the breeze.
A rainbow yawns, extends its arms,
Inviting all to share its charms.

The toaster jumps, pops out some cheer,
A slice of joy is always near.
With sprinkles flying from the sky,
Palettes of laughter soaring high.

Eternal gleam, not quite so clear,
It wraps us up, keeps joy near.
In twirls of whimsy, let's align,
For goofy hearts, in moments divine.

Veils of Illumination

There's a pancake flipping in the air,
With syrup trails, it takes a dare.
The fork looks on, with envy bright,
As it dreams of joining this sweet flight.

A turtle sporting a miniskirt,
Does the cha-cha, oh what a flirt!
While fireflies roll like tiny cars,
Chasing each other among the stars.

The moon steals laughs, with pranks galore,
Tickles the night with a feathered roar.
Each twinkle winks, a wink so bold,
In this luminous dance, worth its weight in gold.

Veils of glow, whimsical and bright,
We dance and twirl in sheer delight.
For here resides a playful sight,
As laughter blooms in endless light.

The Whispering Radiance

In the glow of the lamp, I trip on my shoe,
My shadow bursts out laughing, it knows what I do.
The moon winks at me from a cozy high chair,
While the stars shuffle cards without a single care.

The beams of the lantern whisper silly jokes,
With giggles and snickers from giggling folks.
Even the nightingale sings a tune not right,
As I dance with my shadow in the calm of the night.

Forever Dance of the Fireflies

A firefly winks, saying, 'Catch me if you can!'
But I just end up hugging the nearest fan.
They flit around like they're stars on a spree,
While I'm left clapping, 'Look, one landed on me!'

We twirl in circles, a glow-in-the-dark race,
As lightning bugs teach us how to find space.
Their laughter is magic, it tickles my chin,
As I slide through the garden, a light-headed win.

Brilliance Along the Infinite Path

There's a path made of glitter that leads to a pie,
I skip and I hop, trying not to fly.
The trees whisper secrets, they tickle my ears,
While squirrels address me with comical cheers.

As I wander with purpose, my hat's in a spin,
A rabbit runs past me, he's wearing a grin.
On this sparkly trail, we're all friends tonight,
Chasing dreams that are silly and filled with delight.

Beacon of the Dreams Unchained

There's a lighthouse that's flipping pancakes in waves,
With dreams full of syrup for all the brave knaves.
Seagulls join in with a comedic flap,
While jellyfish dance in a pancake-shaped nap.

With laughter and light, we all take a bite,
As shadows play tag beneath the bright light.
Even the ocean giggles, splashing around,
As we feast on our dreams without a care found.

Boundless Radiance

A bulb blew up in my room,
I thought it was doom.
But the glow filled the air,
It made me want to dance like a bear.

Sunshine on a jam-packed bus,
Makes everyone look like they're in a fuss.
Shadows are chasing the kids,
While the driver pretends to be a whiz.

My cat thinks she's a star,
Under the sun, she dreams of a car.
The grass tickles her paws,
As she purrs and rolls with no flaws.

Twinkle lights in the fridge at night,
Illuminate leftovers with delight.
Even veggies wear a tamarind
Wishing they could be unhinged from this bland.

Infinity's Embrace

Caught in a loop of endless snacks,
Chasing crumbs like endless tracks.
I swear I saw my chips surf,
Riding waves of dip with great verve.

Balloons floating high and grand,
They look lost, but it's all planned.
They laugh as they bob and weave,
Just trying to get out without a leave.

My dog thinks he's the sun's best fan,
Chasing beams that run like a man.
He trips over every toy in sight,
Yet claims he's soaring to new heights.

Clouds laugh at my silly ways,
As I dance in the light of sunny rays.
They float by and snicker at me,
Thinking they've got the real glee.

Shimmering Infinity

The disco ball in my kitchen spins,
Reflecting laughter and silly grins.
The toast pops up like a hasty cheer,
As the cat twirls in her own sphere.

When I trip on my own shoelaces,
I catch giggles from all the faces.
The mirror laughs as I stumble and sway,
Reminding me of a very bright day.

My socks are a carnival, who knew?
Stripes and dots that dance like a crew.
Each time I walk, they celebrate too,
Creating a party for just me and you.

Even the clock joins in the fun,
Ticking its tune, a rhythmic run.
It stops for a moment, then spins a tale,
Of all the baked goods that will never fail.

The Unfading Horizon

The horizon calls with a quirky grin,
Reminding me of the light within.
I chase the sunset on rollerblades,
Until I trip and my laughter cascades.

With a twist and a twirl, the stars appear,
Winking at me, oh so sincere.
They're plotting mischief from way up high,
As I wave back, feeling spry.

A squirrel steals my sandwich, oh dear,
Yet I can't stay mad; it's all in good cheer.
We share a moment, just two pals,
Underneath the dancing, giggling gales.

As the moon rises with a big silly face,
I dance the night away, just in case.
With every twinkle that lights the sky,
I laugh at how time can take flight and fly.

Infinity's Glow

In a world made of sparkles and rays,
A cat tried to catch them for days.
She leaped with a twist,
Missed the glow, what a tryst!

Butterflies giggle and zoom by,
Waving their wings, oh my, oh my!
They dance in the air,
Without a single care.

A duck in shades takes a stroll,
With style, it plays the bold role.
Quacking a tune,
Under the bright moon.

Llamas wear hats, oh what a sight,
Under the shimmer, all feels so right.
They prance and they sway,
In pure, silly play.

Celestial Embrace

The stars play peek-a-boo at night,
While the moon winks, oh what a sight.
A giggle from space,
They dance with such grace.

Comets race, with tails that flare,
Making wishes float through the air.
A cupcake on Mars,
Strawberry with stars!

Asteroids spin in a funky way,
As aliens jive and sway.
In this cosmic place,
Who needs a space race?

With every twinkle and beam,
They weave a whimsical dream.
So grab your best friends,
Let laughter ascend!

Radiant Vistas

Mountains made of candy so sweet,
Where gummy bears dance on their feet.
They skip and they hop,
With lollipops, they stop.

Rivers of chocolate, what a delight,
Flowing and bubbling, such a sight.
With marshmallow boats,
They sing silly notes.

Sunshine in glasses, sipping on tea,
A squirrel joins in, quite carefree.
He wears a bow tie,
With a wink and a sigh.

The hills roll like dough, oh so round,
They bounce and they giggle, so profound.
In this joyful land,
It's silly and grand!

Unbroken Dawn

Morning breaks with a playful grin,
Where puppies leap and joy begins.
They chase after light,
In such morning delight.

Birds wear hats made of toast,
Singing songs, they love the most.
With each chirp and peep,
They wake from their sleep.

Sunflowers dance in the day,
As if they too want to play.
With petals that wave,
Like a bright, sunny rave.

Laughter rolls like a gentle breeze,
Bringing smiles, it's sure to please.
In this wacky morn,
Our hearts are reborn!

Radiance Beyond the Horizon

The sun slipped on a banana peel,
Laughing loudly, what a steal!
Bright rays danced, a cheeky play,
Winking at clouds in a funny way.

Shadows giggled, tripped, and rolled,
Chasing fireflies, oh so bold!
Twilight's chuckle filled the air,
As stars burst forth without a care.

A comet slipped, oh what a show,
Whistling tunes, too fast to slow!
Each twinkle wore a goofy hat,
Grinning at night, imagine that!

In this world of silly cheer,
The light's so bright, you just can't sneer!
With every glow, a laugh is found,
As joy and giggles whirl around.

Luminous Whispers of Dawn

A rooster crowed in a disco beat,
The rays of morn gave him a seat.
Shining bright with hues of cheer,
They painted smiles from ear to ear.

The rabbits bounced, a waltz in view,
With fluffy tails, they danced anew.
Chirping birds joined the fun parade,
In morning's glow, no plans delayed.

Sunbeams tickled the sleepy trees,
As squirrels giggled on the breeze.
Nature's laughter rang so clear,
Chasing away each hint of fear.

With every dawn, the pranks unfold,
In softest light, brave tales told.
So toast the sun with orange juice,
For silly times we won't refuse!

Eternal Glimmer in the Void

In a galaxy, oh so wide,
Stars threw jokes from side to side.
A black hole winked, then made a joke,
"Why don't scientists trust the sun? It's always up to
something!"

Planets spun in a clumsy dance,
With asteroids in a silly prance.
The comets zoomed with wild delight,
"Catch me if you can!" they said, so bright!

Nebulas twirled in colors wild,
Whispering secrets like a child.
Each twinkle shared a laugh or two,
In the dark void, what a view!

Gravity shot a pun to Mars,
"Let's weigh our options, friends, in bars!"
In this space of cosmic jest,
The glimmering lights are truly blessed.

Infinity's Gentle Glow

A light bulb flickered in a quirky way,
Hoping to brighten up the day.
It giggled, and cracked a joke,
"I'm sure it's dark, or smoke broke!"

Candle flames did a little dance,
Flickering soft in a merry trance.
They winked at shadows on the wall,
As laughter echoed in the hall.

Street lamps chatted, shining bright,
Competing over who's the best light.
"Hey, I am the brightest here!"
"Not with that style, oh dear, oh dear!"

With every glow in this giggle fest,
It's a funny world, surely blessed.
Chasing shadows, spreading cheer,
In this glow, we'll persevere!

Whispering Stardust

In the night, stars play peek-a-boo,
Twinkling bright like a silly shoe.
They giggle softly, a cosmic jest,
Making wishes that feel like a quest.

A comet zooms, with a wink and a grin,
It tickles the moon, makes the dark spin.
Galaxies clap, a sparkly parade,
Each twirl of light, a sweet charade.

A star sneezes, like a loud honk honk,
Leaving trails of giggles, a glowing conk.
With each twinkle, a joke's in the air,
Laughter and shimmer together, a flare.

So let's dance under this glittery shower,
As laughter blooms, brightening each hour.
With cosmic chuckles shining so bright,
Who needs the dark when we've got this light?

Daybreak's Promise

The sun pops up like a toasty bun,
Sizzling softly, oh what fun!
Coffee brews in a morning fright,
As sleepy heads scramble for light.

Birds chirp jokes in the dawn's embrace,
Fluffy clouds take the sun's place.
With each giggle, the day takes flight,
Turning yawns into laughter, so bright.

The dew drops dance, a shiny prank,
Playing tag on the garden plank.
Every ray is a tickle on skin,
Waking the world for a cheeky spin.

So grab your shades, let's beat the heat,
With sunny jokes, life's a treat.
In this bright world where we take a stand,
Laughter awakens the joyous land.

Boundless Brilliance

The universe winks in silly ways,
With planets spinning in goofy plays.
A star triplets, in three twinkly lines,
Joking around in spirally designs.

Nebulas puff like giant balloons,
Filling the sky with colorful tunes.
Each puff is a chuckle, a cosmic laugh,
Lighting up dreams like a silly gaffe.

Shooting stars on a joyride dash,
Making wishes and a zippy splash.
With every glide, they giggle with glee,
What a party in infinity's spree!

So let's travel through this groovy space,
With starlit giggles, we quicken the pace.
In the realm of laughter, we'll soar and sway,
Boundless brilliance lights up our way!

Cosmic Luminescence

In the dark, a slipper-sized moon,
Dances with stars, humming a tune.
With every shine, a playful jest,
Who knew space could be so blessed?

Asteroids chuckle, rolling in style,
In cosmic shoes, they prance a while.
Each twist and turn, a light-hearted game,
Glowing bright with laughter, never the same.

Galaxies swirl with a giggly spin,
Each star a grin, let the fun begin!
Radiance flows like a fizzy drink,
In the sparkling sea where we blink and wink.

So let's float in this joy-filled sea,
With cosmic laughter, just you and me.
For in this universe, so wild and free,
The light of laughter shines endlessly!

The Everlasting Flame

In a world where torches glow,
Flickering flames put on a show.
S'mores on sticks, they roast and dance,
Cheesy jokes in a campfire trance.

A candle's wink might start a spark,
Light bulb laughs brighten up the dark.
We debate if it's wax or air,
Who knew that glow can bring such flair?

A disco ball that spins with glee,
Lighting up the whole jamboree.
Dance moves born from shiny beams,
All while the fire pops and screams.

When light's around, why frown or pout?
Just bask in joy and twist about.
So grab a friend, let laughter reign,
Together we'll make a lighted chain.

Ethereal Rays of Hope

Sunbeams peek through morning fog,
Waking up the sleepy dog.
He yawns wide, looks at the sun,
Is it a ray or just a pun?

Clouds float by like fluffy sheep,
They tickle the skies and make me leap.
Here comes a rainbow, what a tease,
It's like nature's way to say, "Say cheese!"

With every glimmer, giggles sprout,
Sunshine on a cold day, there's no doubt.
A parade of rays, a funny sight,
Who knew warmth could be such delight?

So gather 'round, let's share some fun,
Under the glow of everyone.
With sparks of joy that leap and bounce,
We'll chase the shadows and laugh, renounce.

Infinite Radiance in Time

Tick-tock goes the clock of fate,
Glowing hands that never hesitate.
Can't catch the light as it zips by,
But oh, we'll try with a wink and a sigh.

Days may pass like a comic strip,
We stumble on with a goofy slip.
Time and shine, what a quirky clash,
Giggles mixed with a bright flash.

From dawn to dusk, the sun may tease,
Tickling skies with humor, if you please.
We'll trip on shadows, dance on rays,
What better way to spend our days?

So gather 'round the shining grind,
Let's laugh at how bright can be blind.
With every second, make it right,
Our friendships glow, what a silly sight!

Woven Threads of Shine

In a tapestry of merry beams,
We stitch together our goofy dreams.
Laughing as we weave each line,
Creating joy that's simply divine.

Threads of humor, colors bright,
Woven carefully, side by side.
With each tug and a playful tug,
Out comes a grin, snug as a bug.

A patch of silly, a stitch of fun,
We craft our moments 'til we run.
Let's not unravel, hold on tight,
In this fabric, we find delight.

So raise a glass to the yarns we share,
For glistening bonds, beyond compare.
As we craft joy with every rhyme,
In our hearts, they will shine sublime.

Shine Beyond Shadows

In a world where ducks wear shades,
And bees steal honey from the glades.
Light flickers like a joyful sprite,
Who knew the dark could be so bright?

Chasing squirrels in a hare's parade,
While giggles drift in sunlit cascade.
Clouds do a dance, all fluffy and free,
What a sight to see, just wait for me!

The moon in denim, what a surprise,
Winks at the stars with glittering eyes.
With every laugh, the shadows flee,
Dancing shadows, come join our spree!

So dust off your shoes, let's twirl around,
In pools of giggles, we all are bound.
Playful beams in every nook,
Adventure awaits, let's take a look!

The Radiant Passage

A squirrel with shades on a summer spree,
Brings laughter to all as it climbs a tree.
Twinkling moments, let's dive headfirst,
Into sunlit waters, where giggles burst!

Fireflies stutter like they're on a path,
Chasing the breeze, causing smiles to laugh.
The world is quirky, funny, and bright,
Let's jump through joy, oh, what a sight!

With shadows behind, we'll prance and preen,
Like kittens in hats, it's a funny scene.
Every twist and turn, a cheerful embrace,
In golden laughter, we find our place!

So grab a star, let's twirl it and sing,
In this radiant romp, we'll find everything.
With each sparkle we make, the shadows shift,
In our zany world, it's all a gift!

Celestial Flourish

A starfish wearing fancy shoes,
Struts across beaches, enjoying the views.
Waves giggle gently, tickling the feet,
As nature and laughter dance to the beat!

Floating balloons in colors so bright,
Chase after rainbows that tickle our sight.
With silly grins that even clouds share,
Who knew the moon could turn this flair?

Footprints in sand that jump and play,
Seeking mischief in the sun's ballet.
Witty whispers, a cosmic tease,
You'll laugh so hard; it's sure to please!

So let's create a world, silly and loud,
Where every giggle makes shadows proud.
With every twinkle that graces the sky,
We'll shine together, you and I!

Glowing Beyond Boundaries

A cat in a cape, chasing its tail,
Frolics through flowers with laughter so frail.
Tickling the daisies, oh, what a sight,
As colors collide in pure delight!

The sun wears sunglasses, cool as a breeze,
While clouds in pajamas do as they please.
Moonbeams giggle, casting a glow,
Making mischief, saying, 'Let's go!'

Puppies in bowties, ready to prance,
Dancing through gardens in a silly dance.
With each twinkling step, we break the mold,
Let's light up the world, be brave and bold!

So grab your friend, let's shine and play,
In the glow of laughter, we'll brighten the day.
With every chuckle, the shadows retreat,
In our playful glow, life's truly sweet!

Infinite Reflections

In a mirror I see my face,
Just a wink and it's out of place.
Dancing shadows all around,
Chasing giggles, laughter found.

Sunshine plays on my hair,
Winds that swirl without a care.
Playing tag with clouds so white,
Who knew joy could be so light?

Frogs are croaking in a band,
Jiving silly, hand in hand.
Infinite echoes in the air,
Each one laughing without a care.

Catch a giggle in a jar,
Whistle bright, you're a shining star!
When the day blends into night,
Magic blooms, and it feels so right.

Gleaming Eternity

A disco ball reflects the sun,
Spinning wildly, oh what fun!
Rainbow colors, all aglow,
Tiptoe lightly, heel to toe.

Silly hats upon our heads,
Wiggly lines on giant beds.
Chasing dreams that hop and play,
Laughter greets the light of day.

Tickled toes in warm sunshine,
Sunbeams dancing, oh so fine.
Every corner gleams and glows,
Where the humor freely flows.

Giggles echo down the street,
With each laugh, our hearts compete.
In this cheerful, bright parade,
Every moment, joy we've made.

The Illumined Journey

On a train of funky vibes,
Traveling where silliness thrives.
Balloons bouncing, what a sight,
Spreading joy with all our might.

Rainbows sprout from every door,
Chasing puddles, hear them roar!
Stomp and splash, oh what delight,
Colorful dreams take off in flight.

With a giggle, the stars align,
Tickling clouds, it feels divine.
Every bump is a laugh anew,
Who knew journeys could feel like a brew?

Butterflies in bright parade,
Chanting cheers, they serenade.
Joyful whispers from the road,
Carry us with every ode.

Beyond the Bright

Underneath the shining skies,
Where every funny detail lies.
Jellybeans and candy canes,
Laughter dances like the trains.

Bouncing bubbles lift me high,
Making wishes as they fly.
Chasing shadows, giggles flow,
In this world, we steal the show.

Twirling dancers in the light,
Every twirl brings pure delight.
Find a friend and share a joke,
Let the joy around you soak.

Sunset whispers with a grin,
Promises of joy within.
With each memory that ignites,
We'll keep laughing, reaching heights.

The Unbroken Spectrum

Colors collide in a goofy dance,
Rainbows giggle, they take a chance.
A blue cow winks, a green giraffe,
Chasing shadows, look at that laugh!

Prismatic cats chase the sunbeam,
Wobbling around, they munch on cream.
With every hue, a silly grin,
In this wild world, let fun begin!

Jellybean skies in a lollipop shade,
Cloud-people slip in their candy parade.
Bouncing around, no frowns in sight,
Join the party of pure delight!

A kaleidoscope spins; let's twirl and sway,
In this funny place, we'll laugh all day.
Life is a canvas, splashed with fun,
In this spectrum, we're never done!

Luminescence Through the Ages

Once upon a time, in a glittery place,
Dinosaurs danced with a silly grace.
A T-Rex trying to hula hoop,
What a sight, oh what a scoop!

Medieval knights with neon swords,
Frolicking past, breaking all the hoards.
They trade their armor for disco gear,
Jousting on roller skates, oh dear!

The Renaissance crew with their glowing quill,
Painting the skies, oh what a thrill!
Twirling in togas beneath the moon,
With artists laughing, it's quite the tune!

Millennia pass, still glowing bright,
Futures filled with a cosmic light.
From cavemen's fires to stars above,
We laugh through time, what a joyful love!

Glowing Horizons of Possibility

Out beyond the hills where giggles grow,
Silly creatures in a bright, fun show.
A unicorn jumps on a trampoline,
Bouncing so high, it's like a dream!

The sun wears shades, a sight so grand,
With fluffy clouds, we make a band.
A saxophone-singing snail with flair,
Keeps everyone laughing without a care!

A world full of jesters and twinkling lights,
Playing hopscotch on the moonlight nights.
With boundless joy, we find our way,
In the land of laughter, where we play!

Jelly-filled stars and glittery streams,
Chasing our hopes, fulfilling our dreams.
Every sunset dances, a mirthful sight,
In this glowing realm, our spirits take flight!

A Journey Through the Aurora

In the sky where the colors prance,
Dancing lights in a silly romance.
Winking fairies in pajamas bright,
Spinning around, oh what a sight!

Penguins in tuxedos rule the night,
Twirling and sliding, they're full of delight.
They invite us to join their frosty ball,
Where everyone's laughing, having a ball!

Fluffy clouds, like marshmallows, float,
Whispering secrets, they giggle and gloat.
Each twinkling star shares a funny tale,
Of cosmic pranks and interstellar mail!

Through the auroras, we skip and glide,
Wrapped in laughter, we'll never hide.
In this whimsical ride, let's all unite,
On this journey of joy, it's all so bright!

Iridescent Memories

In the attic of my mind, it's clear,
I find old socks and a rubber deer.
Laughter echoes from the past,
Where moments shine, forever cast.

A jelly bean that jumped one day,
Decided it would dance and sway.
It twirled around with such delight,
A candy star in silly flight.

The crayons argue on the floor,
About who's brightest, wanting more.
But peeking through that wooden door,
Is laughter seen, forevermore.

When memories glow like disco balls,
And shadowed kitchens echo calls.
With every giggle, every sigh,
A spark ignites, never to die.

The Luster of Infinity

A squirrel with shades plans a new heist,
To steal all seeds and toast them nice.
While pondering snacks that shine like gold,
He dreams of treasures yet untold.

The moon smells like peanut butter cookies,
As stars wink down, those little rookies.
Each twinkle tells a funny tale,
Of space squirrels on a grand scale.

Time strolls by in polka dot shoes,
With candy canes and colorful hues.
It dances on the tip of a tooth,
Painting the world in whims and truth.

Count the giggles, share each grin,
In this vast cosmos, let's begin.
Every chuckle, a comet's flight,
Sailing through the tickling night.

Luminosity of the Soul

My cat wears a crown made of tin,
Claims the throne with a regal grin.
She paws at dreams upon the rug,
While dust bunnies dance, snug as a bug.

Each thought sparkles like a firefly,
Flitting past as the evening sighs.
In the cupboard, the cupcakes plot,
To stage a coup in this old spot.

The walls have ears, or so I think,
They giggle loud, till my pen goes ink.
Inside my heart, a laughter ball,
Kicking joy through the shadowed hall.

Sometimes the stars play peek-a-boo,
Winking down at a world so blue.
With each chuckle, souls ignite,
Painting joy with pure delight.

The Lasting Spark

A toaster plays a tune at dawn,
While bread dances like a happy fawn.
Jam jars jiggle on the shelf,
As breakfast parties in good health.

Grandpa's jokes, they crack and pop,
Like fireworks, they never stop.
Each punchline twinkles in the air,
Removing all the daily cares.

The tea kettle whistles like a song,
While biscuits munch and sing along.
Spoons have rhythm, forks keep beat,
In this chaotic, tasty seat.

As laughter's spark flickers and glows,
It lights my path wherever it goes.
With every jest, my heart takes flight,
In this twinkling, joyful night.

The Constant Glow

In the fridge, a bright delight,
Leftover pizza shines so bright.
It glimmers all throughout the night,
Encouraging midnight snackers to take flight.

The traffic lights do dance and sway,
As drivers honk and shout, "No way!"
But still, they guide us on our way,
With antics on this busy day.

A bulb that flickers, what a tease,
Playing hide and seek with ease.
It lights my path but makes me sneeze,
At least it's not a bunch of bees!

So here we are, with beams so bright,
Creating laughter, pure delight.
In every glow, find joy tonight,
Unplug and dance in the moonlight!

Spectrums of Eternity

A rainbow's here with goofy flair,
Dancing colors in the air.
A leprechaun? No, it's unfair!
Just nature's palette, everywhere!

Then comes the sun, a golden coin,
For sunburns, it will surely join.
It loves to blast, we can't disjoint,
While we're outside, it's full-on groin!

The stars above, like popcorn spread,
Each little light may be misled.
Some say it's wishes, dreams we fed,
But I just think they're crabby bread.

So when you gaze at night's delight,
Remember they are having a fight.
A comet zips, an asteroid's bite,
In this cosmic jest, we find our light!

Celestial Illuminations

A candle winks, a playful jest,
Her waxy friend thinks he's the best.
He flickers left, then darts to rest,
While shadows join this zany fest.

The moon, a cheese ball in the sky,
Cheddar or brie? We can't deny.
It grins at all the stars nearby,
As they ballet with a twinkling high.

Fireflies buzzing, doing their thing,
Like tiny fairies that dance and sing.
Yet when they fade, what joy they bring,
Their glow makes up for everything!

So gather 'round, you light-filled dreams,
In luminous laughs, life surely beams.
In every sparkle, joy redeems,
Connecting hearts with glowing gleams!

Light Unveiled

In a room, a lamp did fight,
With a shadow in the night.
It flickered, winked, and then it glowed,
Saying, "I'm the star of this abode!"

The cat looked up, with eyes so wide,
Thought the lamp was a UFO from which to hide.
It's just a bulb, don't be a fool,
Now let's all giggle, it's a light-filled school!

They danced around, this merry crew,
As beams bounced off, in silly view.
The dog jumped up, barking so loud,
"I'm the brightest! Bow to your cloud!"

A waltz of bulbs, a playful fight,
In a disco of laughter, pure delight.
For every flicker, there's a smile,
This glowing charade makes life worthwhile!

The Luminous Journey

On a bike with wheels so bright,
I pedaled through the golden light.
I wore a helmet made of cheese,
To keep the thoughts from flying free!

The sun said, "Hey, let's play a game!",
I grinned back, "I'm kind of lame!"
But off we rode, a sillier sight,
As shadows danced in playful flight!

We tripped on beams and bumps of fun,
Each giggle brighter than the sun.
The clouds joined in, tossed a dare,
"Who can float the highest air?"

So, we soared up, through glee and cheer,
With sparkles sparkled bright and near.
The journey was odd, but what a blast,
In a world so bright, we forgot the past!

A Symphony of Radiance

Gather 'round, the bulbs are here,
With a faulty tune, let's lend an ear.
A toaster starts the upbeat fun,
Pops up toast and sings, "Let's run!"

The fridge joins in, with humming glee,
I swear that light just winked at me!
The kettle whistles a high note clear,
"A symphony, let's drink some cheer!"

There's rhythm in the twinkle's glow,
As daylight dances to and fro.
The windows laugh with every beam,
Reflecting dreams, a light-filled theme!

So grab your pens, let's write this song,
Of sparkly moments where we belong.
A melody bright, with a giggle tight,
In this radiant realm, everything's right!

Unfading Visions

In a world of glow and bright embrace,
Where wacky shadows take the place.
A pencil wanders, drawing cheer,
Sketching a llama with a pirate's gear!

The sun sneezed, "Bless you!" said the moon,
With a wink, "Here comes my cartoon!"
Stars twinkled tales of mischief and fun,
As fish on bikes said, "Let's run!"

The laughter grew, in vibrant rays,
As sight became a sweet malaise.
Unfading visions in silly loops,
Colors danced with swings and hoops!

So here we are, with giggles bright,
In a realm where dreams take flight.
With every laugh, the world aligns,
In a glow that twists, and brightly shines!

Allure of the Eternal

A glow in the fridge, what a sight,
Who knew the leftovers could bring delight!
I'm not sure if it's the cheese or the cake,
But it dances like stars on a plate, for goodness sake!

The sun shines bright on my morning toast,
It's butter and jam that I love the most.
The rays whisper secrets, oh what a tease,
Making breakfast feel like such a breeze!

A lamp in the room did a little jig,
As I told my cat she was getting big.
With flickering bulbs and a wink of the eye,
We laughed as the shadows slid by, oh my!

In the moonlight, my socks took flight,
Dancing shoes that shine through the night.
My dog rolled his eyes, what a sight to behold,
As I twirled with my socks in a dance, oh so bold!

When Light Meets Eternity

Two fireflies buzz in the dusk's embrace,
Chasing their dreams in a wild race.
They blink and they flash, what a silly affair,
Glowing like stars with not a single care.

Why did the lightbulb break? Oh, dear!
It couldn't take the pressure, that much is clear.
It tried to be bright, but just couldn't stand,
So I made it a hat from an old rubber band!

I found a flashlight under my bed,
Started a party, lit up my head!
With shadows that danced and giggles galore,
Who knew having fun was a chore to explore?

The sun took a peek through a window pane,
And I laughed louder than a runaway train.
"Is it time to wake up?" it seemed to say,
"Or just to join in my wacky play?"

The Dazzling Continuum

A disco ball hung from my mom's old hat,
Reflecting the rays while I danced with the cat.
Round and round in a glorious twirl,
Her whiskers a-swish, oh what a whirl!

The rainbow appeared just after the rain,
It winked at the clouds as they went down the drain.
So I grabbed my crayons and drew it all out,
With splashes of colors that made me shout!

The candlelight flickered like it was shy,
As I tried to impress with my best pie in the sky.
But it melted away, oh what a scene,
Leaving me craving, and that's just mean!

In the hallway, my shadow did glide,
Doing a cha-cha, with such silly pride.
With giggles and glares, we put on a show,
As the walls laughed along with our glow!

Glimmers of the Cosmos

A comet dashed past, wearing a hat,
Chasing the stars in a whimsical spat.
"Oh what a ride!" said the moon with a grin,
"Just don't forget where you've been!"

Starlight spilled like syrup on toast,
While I attempted to make the cat my host.
With treats and a wink, it turned up its nose,
And danced in delight, no need for the prose.

The galaxy laughed at my spinning chair,
I declared it a rocket! "Hold on, if you dare!"
But my coffee went flying, oh what a sight,
As I soared through the room in outrageous delight.

My socks glimmered bright with stars made of fluff,
While I twirled around like I'd had too much stuff.
In a cosmic ballet of joy and of fun,
Who needs a spaceship when you've got sunlight run?

Timeless Luminescence

In the fridge glows my leftover pie,
Radiating joy, oh my, oh my!
I wonder if it counts as a meal,
Or just a snack that makes me squeal.

A lamp in the corner starts to hum,
That funky dance is quite the sum!
Chasing shadows, giving them a fright,
Who knew bulbs could party all night?

When I spill milk, it shines like the stars,
A cosmic splash on my kitchen bars!
It twinkles and sparkles, what a mess!
But it's a good mess, I must confess.

So raise a toast to all that gleams,
Even if it's just our silly dreams.
With laughter and giggles, let's ignite,
This glowing life, oh what a sight!

Forever Bright

My dog found a glow stick, what a treat,
He looks like a cross between cute and neat!
Chasing shadows like some bright knight,
Barking at breezes, oh what a sight!

The moon's wearing sunglasses tonight,
Too cool to shine, it's out of sight!
Stars wink at me, a celestial jest,
"Do I really have to glow?" they jest!

In the corner, dust bunnies dance,
Oh what a party, they prance and prance!
With twinkling eyes, they laugh with delight,
Who knew dust could throw such a night?

So here's to moments that make us smile,
Life's little quirks, brightening our while.
With each chuckle, we spark the right,
In this wild ride we call the night!

Celestial Dances

The toaster pops, a golden toast,
It did a jig, and I laughed the most!
With butter melting in a twirl,
That's breakfast time in a sugary whirl!

The cat thinks the light is a new toy,
Pouncing and bouncing, oh what a joy!
It sneaks like a ninja, oh what a sight,
Stealthily glowing in the dim light!

Fireflies are auditioning for a role,
In a wacky play, they grab my soul.
They flash their cues, but miss their lines,
Still more entertaining than ten comedians' signs!

We dance beneath this sparkling show,
With laughter echoing high and low.
Join the fun at this starry height,
Under the skies, everything's bright!

The Unseen Glow

My socks have a glow, or maybe it's dirt,
Eagerly dipping in colors that flirt!
An unseen spark of fashion's delight,
Who needs a runway when you're this bright?

The microwave beeps with a giggle inside,
Like it knows secrets, oh how it pried!
A meal that's mutated, a science fair feat,
Glow-in-the-dark spaghetti, quite the treat!

Sunflowers nodding in a quirky dance,
Waving at bees who can't help but prance!
In a world that sparkles, let's take a flight,
To chase joy, and give darkness a fright!

So let your smile be the beacon today,
Light up the moments, come what may!
With giggles and sparkles, we'll unite,
Creating magic, oh what a sight!

Radiance Unbound

In the morning, I trip on the sun,
It shines so bright, it's having fun.
My toast is glowing, what a sight,
It yells, 'Breakfast, with extra light!'

The fridge hums a cheerful tune,
As shadows dance beneath the moon.
With each sip of my glowing tea,
I swear it winked at me with glee.

My socks are bright, all mismatched hues,
They laugh and tease, refusing to lose.
In a world where colors dance and play,
Even the ceiling has things to say.

So come and join this luminous spree,
Where shadows shout and glow, oh me!
Radiance isn't just for the skies,
It's in our hearts, and giggles, and pies!

Enduring Brilliance

Every bulb in the house is a star,
Glowing with stories from near and far.
I flipped the switch; they did a jig,
Even the old lamp is now a big pig!

In the kitchen, the fridge gleams bright,
It's holding mysteries of leftover bites.
Each time I peek, it winks and beams,
Making me laugh with its food-filled dreams.

The cat paints rainbows with each little pounce,
While the sun's rays play and bounce.
With glittering sparkles on the ground,
The floor's a disco, aren't we all wound?

With lights that flicker and brighten the day,
Even our troubles just dance away.
In this glow, where joy compiles,
We'll find the funny in endless miles!

A Tapestry of Stars

A quilt of glimmers stitched with care,
Stars giggle softly, a light affair.
They tease the moon, a shiny ball,
Whispering wishes to each late-night call.

In the park, streetlamps sway and quake,
Dancing shadows, what a riot they make!
The turtles blink, caught in the show,
While the night blooms in a radiant flow.

The fireflies join with their little flare,
Like tiny jesters, they light the air.
Each twinkling laugh fills the vast night,
With happy chaos, it feels just right.

Laughter and glow in the fabric of dreams,
Even the car horns produce happy screams.
In this endless canvas, bright and vast,
We find the funny in joys that last!

The Light that Never Fades

Once upon a time, I found a gleam,
It giggled and sparkled, like a wild dream.
I tried to catch it, ran with delight,
But it tickled me, taking flight.

I looked in the mirror; my hair was aflame,
Turns out beauty has a funny game.
Each strand of light danced with pride,
As laughter echoed, traveling wide.

The clock in the corner shimmers and chimes,
Saying silly things like it's lost in times.
With jokes in every tick and tock,
It keeps me smiling, a funny clock!

So here's to the glow that fills up the air,
With chuckles and giggles, it's always there.
No dimming down in this joyful trade,
With laughter as bright as a brilliant parade!

Sundrenched Memories and Glowing Futures

In a world where shades retreat,
We dance on rays, oh so sweet.
Chasing shadows, laughing wide,
With sun-kissed joy, we take a ride.

Popsicles melting, sticky hands,
Silly stories, laughter stands.
Each golden hour, a cherished score,
In the glow, we crave for more.

Bubbles floating, taking flight,
In our hearts, a spark so bright.
Chasing giggles through the sun,
Creating tales, oh what fun!

Fleeting moments, we hold tight,
Giggling softly through the night.
With every smile and silly dance,
We find our bliss in sunlit chance.

The Radiant Canvas of Tomorrow.

Brushstrokes bright across the sky,
With a wink and playful sigh.
Colors swirl, a jolly spree,
Artful chaos, wild and free.

Tomorrow's scenes await our cheer,
Filled with joy, and not a fear.
With each dawn, a fresh new laugh,
Splashes bright in our photograph.

Giggles painting the air so loud,
Each moment, a joyful crowd.
We hop on clouds of cotton candy,
In vibrant hues, life's never dandy.

So sprinkle joy on every face,
In this wacky, sunny place.
Hand in hand, we leap and spin,
In our hearts, the game begins.

Eternal Horizons

Waves of laughter crash so bright,
Chasing dreams in morning light.
Every giggle, a distant star,
Navigating our way, bizarre.

With every quirk and silly cheer,
We surf the tides, no room for fear.
The horizon calls, 'Come play with me!'
In this grand adventure, wild and free.

Sundae spills and kite mishaps,
Each moment, a meme that snaps.
Under the sun's watchful eye,
We craft our tales, oh me, oh my!

So let's embrace the absurd twists,
In our laughter, the day persists.
With every sunrise, we ignite,
A world painted in pure delight.

Luminous Whispers

Whispers of giggles in the breeze,
We chase them down with frantic ease.
Each tickle brings a sunny grin,
With every prank, the fun begins.

Glowworms giggle in moonlit play,
Silly secrets shared each day.
Dancing shadows on the lawn,
Our laughter sings the dawn's sweet song.

In the glow of twilight's charm,
We wrap ourselves in joy's warm arm.
With playful pokes and jests we score,
Creating memories to explore.

So gather round, let humor guide,
With radiant hearts, we won't hide.
In each twinkle, a spark of jest,
We find our peace, we find our zest.

Timeless Gleam Across the Skies

A squirrel wore shades, so cool, so bright,
He danced on rooftops, a silly sight.
With acorns as snacks, he'd shimmy and sway,
Chasing the clouds, he'd brighten the day.

A parrot recited poems with flair,
Claiming to know the secrets up there.
He'd argue with kites, oh what a scene,
Debating their purpose, like kings and queens.

The sun played tricks with a wink and a glow,
Juggling the weather, to and fro.
Creating rainbows with laughter so loud,
It soaked the whole world in a colorful shroud.

In this circus of joy, nothing's amiss,
Each moment a giggle, each hour a bliss.
The sky's just a canvas where mischief aligns,
With colors and chuckles, oh how it shines!

Resilience of the Glorious Day

A rooster crowed in the noon's bright hey,
Forgetful of morning, he started to play.
With a tap dance of feathers, he strutted so proud,
Claiming the day, through laughter and crowds.

The clouds formed shapes, a dog and a cat,
One rolled a ball, the other wore a hat.
They played hide and seek amongst the blue skies,
Drawing smiles from onlookers, sparking the spies.

A turtle did yoga, on a sunlit rock,
With a zen-like focus, he held every block.
Cheering, the fish flipped in synchronized cheer,
In this splendid play, worries disappeared.

Amidst all the giggling, the world found its stride,
With warmth in their hearts, and laughter as pride.
Every inch of the day felt oddly misplaced,
Yet joy filled the air; it couldn't be chased!

Sunbeams in the Veil of Darkness

The moon wore sunglasses, a sight to behold,
Sipping on starlight, feeling quite bold.
With shadows as friends, they'd play tag at night,
While the sun slept on, tucked in, far from sight.

A cat with a flashlight was searching for mice,
Yet only found shadows, which weren't very nice.
With each little pounce, he created a mess,
But laughter erupted at his golden distress.

Bats sang karaoke in the depth of the gloom,
Their echoes a chorus, in each darkened room.
While owls hooted back, trying to keep the beat,
Making music from stillness, oh isn't that sweet?

In this dance of the night, where jokes find their way,
The stars twinkled bright, adding to the play.
A tapestry spun from both giggle and fright,
Made magic from shadows and delightful light!

A Tapestry of Reflections

Mirrors in puddles wanted to chat,
Reflecting shy turtles who wore a top hat.
They pondered their purpose in ripples and waves,
Bubbling with laughter, oh how each one braves!

The trees whispered secrets, tickled by breeze,
Sharing tales of travelers and quirky unease.
A raccoon popped out with a comedy act,
Reporting the happenings, keeping it tact.

The sun stretched its fingers through branches above,
Wrapping the world in a warm, gentle glove.
Each ray was a jester, on a bright stage to play,
Spinning tales of wonder to brighten the day.

In this joyous spectacle, humor combined,
With chuckles and giggles, all worry confined.
Underneath it all, light dances so free,
Creating reflections of pure jubilee!